I0156813

Christ the Counselor

Reflections on Jesus as a Therapist

Dr. Max Malikow

Christ the Counselor

Copyright © 2017 by Max Malikow

Permission to use "The Divine Counselor" by Harry Anderson on the front cover given by GoodSalt Christian Art and Photography.

All rights reserved. No part of this book may be reproduced or transmitted in any form or by any means without written permission of the author.

Library of Congress Control Number: 2017952453

ISBN 9780998560632

To Dr. Gordon Fee: Academically, you brought Jesus to life in two exceptional courses: "New Testament Survey" and "The Life of Jesus."

To Brother Frank Guiliano: Your depth, wisdom, and love are comforting and inspiring.

To Dr. Mark Karper: Your suggestion, made in a conversation over lunch, provided the impetus for this book.

To: Dr. Douglas K. Stuart: Your scholarship and humor made Old Testament study informative, memorable, and joyful.

Table of Contents

Acknowledgement

One Solitary Life

He was born in an obscure village, the son of a peasant woman.

He grew up in another village, where he worked in a carpenter's shop until he was thirty. Then for three years he became a wandering preacher.

He never wrote a book. He never held an office. He never had a family or owned a house. He didn't go to college. He never visited a big city. He never travelled two hundred miles from the place where he was born. He did none of those things one usually associates with greatness.

He had no credentials but himself.

He was only thirty-three when the tide of public opinion turned against him. His friends ran away. He was turned over to his enemies and went through a mockery of a trial. He was executed by the state. While he was dying, his executioners gambled for his clothing, the only property he had on earth. When he was dead he was laid in a borrowed grave through the pity of a friend.

Twenty centuries have come and gone, and today he is the central figure of the human race and the leader of mankind's progress. All the armies that ever marched, all the navies that ever sailed, all the parliaments that ever sat, all the kings that ever reigned, put together, have not affected the life of man on this earth as much as that one solitary life.

Revised version of Dr. James Allen Francis' essay, "Arise Sir Knight!" Published in *The Real Jesus and Other Sermons* (1926, Philadelphia, PA: Judson Press, pp. 123-124).

Introduction

No book is intended for everybody. This one was written for lay and professional counselors who are curious about the compatibility of biblically derived counseling principles and contemporary mental health practice. Since Jesus is part of the title two clarifications are in order at the outset. First, this book is not a theological treatise on the person and work of Jesus Christ. A reader anticipating an analysis of Jesus as God incarnate (Christology) or his mission (soteriology) must look elsewhere. Second, neither is this book offered as a commentary. A reader expecting an analysis of biblical texts (exegesis) also must look elsewhere.

This volume draws attention to the competency of Jesus Christ as a counselor and psychotherapist. (Chapter I defines counseling and psychotherapy and distinguishes them from each other.) It was written with confidence that authentic wisdom is found in the teachings of Jesus Christ and such wisdom is bound by neither time nor place. Although the expression, "all truth is God's truth" is associated with the Christian philosopher Arthur Holmes, the concept is not unique to him. Over a generation ago he wrote:

> (I)f God and his wisdom are unchangingly the same, then truth is likewise unchanging and thus *universal*. If all truth is his, and he understands fully its interrelatedness, then truth is *unified* in his perfect

understanding. ...Everything is known to the divine creator, and in his perfect understanding all wisdom and knowledge form an interrelated whole. Truth is one (1977, pp. 8,11).

Social psychologist Jonathan Haidt chose *Finding Modern Truth in Ancient Wisdom* as the subtitle for his book, *The Happiness Hypothesis*. In its introduction he explains the harmony he discovered between ancient wisdom and modern psychological research.

> ... I read dozens of works of ancient wisdom, mostly from the three great zones of classical thought: India ... China ... and the cultures of the Mediterranean. ... I also read a variety of other works of philosophy and literature from the last five hundred years. ... I have drawn on ten ancient ideas and a great variety of modern research findings to tell the best story I can about the causes of human flourishing, and the obstacles to well being that we place in our own paths (2006, pp. x-xi).

Haidt's literary investigation included the Old and New Testaments. The premise of the book you are reading is the wisdom embedded in the teachings of Jesus are compatible with many of the principles of current clinical psychological practice.

When Jesus was engaged in helping someone examine, understand, and possibly change a thought, emotion or behavior he was serving as a therapist - a healer. When providing advice on decision-making or life management he was acting as a counselor. Designating Jesus as a therapist or a counselor is not always a binary choice. In some encounters he served in both capacities. This book consists of ten personal interactions Jesus had with either an individual or a small group. Each is taken from the New Testament, NIV translation (New International Version). Each encounter provides an illustration of a widely accepted clinical principle.

Moreover, this book is intended for those engaged in counseling or psychotherapy, as providers or recipients, who are seeking assurance that there is no necessary conflict between Christian faith and psychological practice. It has been said the function of the church is to comfort the afflicted and afflict the comfortable. Hopefully this treatise will comfort those seeking encouragement that "Christian counseling" is not an oxymoron. And, hopefully, it will unsettle those who are comfortable in their belief that Christian faith is irreconcilable with effective counseling and psychotherapy.

I. How Do Counseling and Psychotherapy Differ?

The beginning of wisdom is the definition of terms.
                                                            - Socrates

George Bernard Shaw wrote, "The single biggest problem in communication is the illusion that it has taken place" (2017). Although this is an overstatement, he recognized people often believe they are communicating when they are not. One explanation for this illusion is an unwitting disagreement on definitions. The classic Abbott and Costello comedy routine "Who's on First?" brilliantly illustrates two people not communicating because they are using the same words with different meanings. Meaningful discussion of an issue requires a shared understanding of key terms. In order to obviate miscommunication by the succeeding chapters, several terms and their definitions are presented in this chapter. No argument is made for any of these definitions being exclusive or irrefutable. Rather, these definitions provide the meaning of specific terms in the context of this book.

psychotherapy

Psychotherapy is engagement with a mental health professional for the purpose of examining, understanding, and possibly changing thoughts, emotions, and/or behaviors. This term is derived from the Greek words for soul (*psuche*) and healing (*therapeia*). The soul is the seat of affections and will, often understood, simply, as a human being.

If the phrase "engagement with a mental health professional" is amended to "engagement with another person" then psychotherapy takes on an expanded meaning. E. Fuller Torrey, a psychiatrist, argued for this expanded meaning in *Witchdoctors and Psychiatrists: The Common Roots of Psychotherapy and Its Future*:

> This book is an attempt to provide a framework for understanding the activities of psychotherapists around the world. ...
>
> This book will focus on the healer. It will attempt to show how much of his effectiveness comes through his sharing of a common worldview with the patient, through certain personality characteristics, and through expectations the patient has of him. It will then show another source of his effectiveness, the techniques of therapy, are basically the same whether they are used by a witchdoctor or a psychiatrist (1986, pp. xiii, xiv).

If the expanded definition is allowed then referring to Jesus as a psychotherapist is appropriate. To refer to Jesus in this way is not irreverent. Neither does it disregard him as a moral teacher, physical healer, miracle worker or as God incarnate and Savior.

counseling

Counseling is advice seeking for the purpose of addressing a life issue. It is distinguished from psychotherapy in that counseling does not address an emotional disorder or mental illness. In the current day, criteria for diagnosing conditions as mental illnesses are found in the American Psychiatric Association's *Diagnostic and Statistical Manual of Mental Disorders* (*Fifth Edition*). A *patient* is an individual with a diagnosed mental disorder engaged in treatment with a mental health professional. A *client* is an individual who has retained a counselor to receive advice for the purpose of addressing a life issue. Examples of counseling in contrast to psychotherapy are deciding whether to divorce, change jobs or transfer colleges.

psychology

Psychology is the "science of behavior and mental processes" (Myers, 2010, p. 6). Psychologist David Myers described psychology's origin with this scenario:

> Once upon a time, on a planet in this neighborhood of the universe, there came to be people. Soon thereafter, these creatures became intensely interested in themselves and in one another: *Who are we? What produces our thoughts? Our actions? And how are we to understand and manage those around us?* (p. 2).

I. How Do Counseling and Psychotherapy Differ?

Curiosity about ourselves and others is a defining feature of the human condition.

psychiatry

Psychiatry is the branch of medicine specializing in the prevention and treatment of mental and emotional disorders. Psychiatrists often provide psychotherapy and counseling. As physicians they can prescribe medications, something psychologists cannot do. (Exceptions are New Mexico and Louisiana, where psychologists can prescribe medications if they are specifically trained in psychopharmacology - "the study of the effects of drugs on mind and behavior ") (p. 660).

II. The Rich Young Man (Luke 18:18-27)
The Yalom Principle

The loss of a possession frees us from it.

- Marty Rubin

18 A certain ruler asked him, "Good teacher, what must I do to inherit eternal life?"
19 "Why do you call me good?" Jesus answered. "No one is good—except God alone.
20 You know the commandments: 'You shall not commit adultery, you shall not murder, you shall not steal, you shall not give false testimony, honor your father and mother.'"
21 "All these I have kept since I was a boy," he said.
22 When Jesus heard this, he said to him, "You still lack one thing. Sell everything you have and give to the poor, and you will have treasure in heaven. Then come, follow me."
23 When he heard this, he became very sad, because he was very wealthy.
24 Jesus looked at him and said, "How hard it is for the rich to enter the kingdom of God!
25 Indeed, it is easier for a camel to go through the eye of a needle than for someone who is rich to enter the kingdom of God."
26 Those who heard this asked, "Who then can be saved?"
27 Jesus replied, "What is impossible with man is possible with God" (Luke 18:18-27).

The eminent psychiatrist Irvin Yalom maintains psychotherapy can be reduced to two questions:

II. The Rich Young Man (Luke 18:18-27)

1. What do you *really* want?
2. Is your current lifestyle moving you closer to or farther from what you say you really want?

The narrative of "The Rich Ruler," found in Luke's gospel (also in Matthew's and Mark's) is an account of Jesus' challenge to a wealthy young man to consider what he *really* wanted. Yalom also maintains that death is one of the four givens relevant to psychotherapy. The ruler, although living a life of material comfort, was uneasy about his ultimate state. He believed "eternal life" was a possibility but was uncertain that he would attain it.

Jesus drew the young man's attention to the Ten Commandments. The ruler responded that he had lived in obedience to them. But instead of reassuring him that he would enter into eternal life, Jesus told him he must go beyond the law: "You still lack one thing. Sell everything you have and give to the poor, and you will have treasure in heaven (eternal life). Then come, follow me (be my disciple)." With these words Jesus challenged him to declare what he *really* wanted. The ruler had said he wanted eternal life; Jesus asked him if he was willing to divest and distribute his wealth to secure it. The value of that which is desired is demonstrated by a willingness to sacrifice for it.

In this narrative Jesus is not declaring divestiture of all material goods as a prerequisite for eternal life. Rather, he perceived the ruler was interested in heaven if it could be attained without sacrifice. Ironically, the ruler had become enslaved to his "possessions" and Jesus offered him liberation.

12

Yalom's principle is observable in this interaction. First, the ruler declared what he wanted. Jesus tested him him to see if he *really* wanted it. In Matthew's account the man is described as departing from Jesus at this point: "When the young man heard this, he went away sad because he had great wealth" (19:22). Yalom's second principle asks if the current lifestyle is consistent with the expressed desire. If they are not compatible then either the lifestyle or the stated desire must be revised.

Yalom's second principle is reminiscent of a concept found in Friedrich Nietzsche's *Thus Spake Zarathustra: A Book for All and None* (1976) Here Nietzsche speaks through an aged prophet, replete with wisdom, who expresses one of Nietzsche's most important ideas: *eternal recurrence*. Presented as a hypothetical question, he asks: What if you were to live the life you are now living again and again throughout eternity - would this change you?

> What if some day or night, a demon were to steal after you into your loneliest loneliness and say to you: "This life as you now live it and have lived it, you will have to live once more and innumerable times more; and there will be nothing new in it, but every pain and every joy and every thought and sigh and everything unutterably small or great in your life will have to return to you, all in the same succession and sequence ... The eternal hourglass of existence is turned upside down again and again, and you with it, speck of dust!" Would you not throw yourself down and gnash your

teeth and curse the demon who spoke thus? Or have you once experienced a tremendous moment when you would have answered him, "You are a god and never have I heard anything more divine." If this thought gained possession of you, it would change you as you are or perhaps crush you (1976, 341).

Yalom has provided the following commentary on *eternal recurrence*:

If you engage in this experiment and find the thought painful or even unbearable, there is one obvious explanation: you do not believe you've lived your life well. I would proceed by posing such questions as, How have you not lived well? What regrets do you have about your life? My purposes not to draw anyone into a sea of regret for the past but, ultimately, to turn his or her gaze toward the future and this potentially life-changing question: *What can you do now in your life so that one year or five years from now, you won't look back and have similar dismay about the new regrets you've accumulated? In other words, can you find a way to live without continuing to accumulate regrets?* (2008, 101).

III. Paying Taxes to Caesar (Matthew 22: 15-22) The Beck Principle

A dilemma is a situation in which no matter what you choose you'll be wrong.

- attributed to Oscar Wilde

15 Then the Pharisees went out and laid plans to trap him in his words.
16 They sent their disciples to him along with the Herodians. "Teacher," they said, "we know that you are a man of integrity and that you teach the way of God in accordance with the truth. You aren't swayed by others, because you pay no attention to who they are.
17 Tell us then, what is your opinion? Is it right to pay the imperial tax to Caesar or not?"
18 But Jesus, knowing their evil intent, said, "You hypocrites, why are you trying to trap me?
19 Show me the coin used for paying the tax." They brought him a denarius,
20 and he asked them, "Whose image is this? And whose inscription?"
21 "Caesar's," they replied. Then he said to them, "So give back to Caesar what is Caesar's, and to God what is God's."
22 When they heard this, they were amazed. So they left him and went away (Matthew 22: 15-22).

The intention of the Pharisees was to discredit Jesus by presenting him with a conundrum. If Jesus said the imperial tax should be paid then he would lose standing in the Jewish community because the Jews despised paying taxes to Rome. If Jesus said the tax should not be paid then he would be on record as inciting rebellion against Caesar and thus a traitor to

Rome. However he answered he was going to be in trouble, precisely what the Pharisees intended.

But was Jesus actually in a situation from which there could be no satisfactory escape? A dilemma is distressing because it requires a choice among unpleasant options. However, the unpleasantness of the options is often a matter of perception. After informing his adversaries that he was on to them, he sagaciously reasoned that the tax issue did not constitute a dilemma. Caesar wanted something God did not want; God desired something in which Caesar had no interest. Rome wanted money and God wanted his people to be obedient to the 613 *mitzvah* (commandments) found in the *Torah* (Pentateuch). Hence, there was no conflict between the two obligations.

The counseling principle operative in this narrative involves misperception. Aaron Beck is the founder of the psychotherapeutic approach known as *Cognitive Behavioral Therapy* (CBT). He is convinced that many psychological disorders are the result of misperceptions. These misperceptions, which he refers to as *cognitive distortions*, lead to illogical conclusions. For example, an individual might hear others laughing when walking by them. "They're laughing at me" is a misperception because someone in the group has just told a very funny joke. This cognitive distortion leads to reinforcement of the belief, "Nobody likes me, I'll never have any friends." Beck believes there are three categories of cognitive distortions: misperceptions about self, others, and the future. Because they are invariably negative, he refers to them as the *negative triad*.

In CBT the therapist challenges misperceptions by asking the patients to justify their beliefs. When they are unable to do so the patients are receptive to alternative beliefs that are more reasonable as well as more optimistic. *Cognitive restructuring* is Beck's term for the presentation of more reasonable alternatives. Jesus engaged in cognitive restructuring in this encounter with the Pharisees. The last verse in the narrative implies their receptivity, their departure notwithstanding: "When they heard this, they were amazed. So they left him and went away" (Matthew 22:22).

The Pharisees had fallen into constricted thinking on the matter of taxes. They believed the payment of taxes would be dishonoring to God. Jesus convincingly argued that God is honored by obedience to his commandments rather than a refusal to give money to Caesar. This is not to say Jesus' opponents were grateful to him for this cognitive restructuring. Nevertheless, he was effective at providing them with a new perspective.

IV. Lord of the Sabbath (Luke 6: 1-11)
The Dalai Lama Principle

Justice is not in the letter of the law, it is in the distribution of love.

- Anonymous

1 One Sabbath Jesus was going through the grainfields, and his disciples began to pick some heads of grain, rub them in their hands and eat the kernels.

2 Some of the Pharisees asked, "Why are you doing what is unlawful on the Sabbath?"

3 Jesus answered them, "Have you never read what David did when he and his companions were hungry?

4 He entered the house of God, and taking the consecrated bread, he ate what is lawful only for priests to eat. And he also gave some to his companions."

5 Then Jesus said to them, "The Son of Man is Lord of the Sabbath."

6 On another Sabbath he went into the synagogue and was teaching, and a man was there whose right hand was shriveled.

7 The Pharisees and the teachers of the law were looking for a reason to accuse Jesus, so they watched him closely to see if he would heal on the Sabbath.

8 But Jesus knew what they were thinking and said to the man with the shriveled hand, "Get up and stand in front of everyone." So he got up and stood there.

9 Then Jesus said to them, "I ask you, which is lawful on the Sabbath: to do good or to do evil, to save life or to destroy it?"

10 He looked around at them all, and then said to the man, "Stretch out your hand." He did so, and his hand was completely restored.

IV. Lord of the Sabbath (Luke 6: 1-11)

11 But the Pharisees and the teachers of the law were furious and began to discuss with one another what they might do to Jesus (Luke 6: 1-11)

Legalism is strict adherence to the law. Legalism is not necessarily a bad thing; good laws deserve obedience. However, strict adherence to unjust laws perpetuates injustice. The Reverend Dr. Martin Luther King, Jr. addressed this in his "Letter from Birmingham Jail" in which he asserted all citizens bear simultaneous responsibilities to obey just laws and disobey those that are unjust. His letter provided a criterion for discerning inequitable laws:

> One may well ask, "How can you advocate breaking some laws and obeying others?" The answer is found in the fact that there are two types of laws: there are just laws, and there are unjust laws. I would agree with St. Augustine that "An unjust law is no law at all." Now, what is the difference between the two? How does one determine when a law is just or unjust? A just law is a man-made code that squares with the moral law, or the law of God. An unjust law is a code that is out of harmony with the moral law. To put it in the terms of St. Thomas Aquinas, an unjust law is a human law that is not rooted in eternal and natural law. Any law that uplifts human personality is just. Any law that degrades human personality is unjust (04/16/1963).

Although rules are not made to be broken, it is sometimes necessary to suspend a rule to serve a greater good. A recent law review article, "When Rules Are Made to Be Broken," describes the dilemma judges face when a bad rule frustrates justice:

> What should a judge do when she expects that applying a straightforward but bad rule will result in an unjust outcome? A judge has two possible ways of dealing with such a situation. First, she may diligently follow the rule, allow the expected unjust outcome, and call attention to the problem in the hope of fixing the rule for future cases. This path presents a dilemma for the judge: the more unfair the outcome, the more likely the call to legislators will be answered; but the more unfair the outcome, the more the judge might want to avoid the responsibility or association with the result. Second, a judge may intentionally misapply the rule to achieve a more just outcome in the instant matter but risk appearing incapable of interpreting and following rules, and worse, increase the risk that the rule will go unfixed, with the knowledge that future applications will likely result in more injustices. The more straightforward and clear the rule is, the less flexibility the judge will have to get away with masquerading a misapplication as legitimate interpret-tation (Eigon, Sherwyn, Ceriale, and Menillo, 2015, pp. 2-3).

Even strict adherence to a good law can be a bad thing when it prevents a greater good. It is this expression of legalism that Jesus encountered when he healed on the

Sabbath. He suspended obedience to the law to serve the intention of the law. Of course, this raises the question: What is the intention of the law, in this case, the Sabbath? In the parallel account in Mark's gospel Jesus said to the Pharisees, "The Sabbath was made for man, not man for the Sabbath" (2: 27). The Sabbath provides one day in seven to rest from labor. Observing the Sabbath is the fourth commandment:

> Remember the Sabbath day by keeping it holy. Six days you shall labor and do all your work, but the seventh day is a Sabbath to the Lord your God. On it you shall not do any work, neither you nor your son or daughter, nor your manservant or maidservant, nor your animals, nor the alien within your gates. For in six days the Lord made the heavens and the earth, the sea, and all that is in them, but he rested on the seventh day. Therefore the Lord blessed the Sabbath day and made it holy (Exodus 20: 8-11).

A day off from work is life enriching. It is physically and spiritually invigorating. This is why the Sabbath was made for man. The intention of all God's commandments is life enrichment. On this occasion Jesus healed on the day of rest, asking rhetorically if it was lawful to do good and save life on the Sabbath. The man whose withered hand was restored benefitted physically and spiritually. His encounter with Jesus left him with a fully functioning hand and grateful heart.

The counseling principle demonstrated in this narrative is the importance of flexibility. Jesus encouraged pliability in applying the commandments when a Pharisee asked him which of the commandments is the greatest.

> Jesus replied, " 'Love the Lord your God with all your heart and with all your soul and with all your mind.' This the first and greatest commandment. And the second is like it, 'Love your neighbor as yourself.' All of the Law and Prophets hang on these two commandments" (Matthew 22: 37-40).

The implication of Jesus' response is the application of the law must be consistent with love for one's neighbor thereby demonstrating love for God. When Jesus denounced the scribes and Pharisees as "blind guides who strain out a gnat and swallow a camel" it was for their meticulous attention to ritual and obtuseness to "the more important matters of the law - justice, mercy, and faithfulness" (23: 23-24).

One of the Dalai Lama's instructions for life is, "Learn the rules so you'll know how to break them properly" (2017). He believes rules must be known and understood if they are to be broken, and if they are to be broken they must be broken properly. This is hardly a cavalier attitude toward the law. Rather, it is instruction to respect the law but to be open to deviating from it under certain conditions. Determining when these conditions exist is often a difficult matter. Nevertheless, at times, counseling and psychotherapy involve encouraging and helping someone to make this determination.

Discerning when a widely accepted law (or commandment or principle) should be suspended is something to be determined individually. There is no algorithm for such decisions owing the variables of person and circumstance. For instance, Eric Liddell sacrificed an almost certain gold medal in the 1924 Olympic games when he refused to compete on the Sabbath. For Liddell, a devout Christian, the Sabbath was a day for worship and reflection. An example of flexibility is Dietrich Bonhoeffer, a German clergyman who actively opposed Adolf Hitler and the Nazis. It is widely believed Bonhoeffer's participation in the German resistance included involvement in a plot to assassinate Hitler, clearly a violation of the sixth commandment. Bonhoeffer believed a failure to take direct action against evil is tantamount to condoning it. Accordingly he wrote:

> If I sit next to a madman as he drives a car into a group of innocent bystanders. I can't, as a Christian, simply wait for the catastrophe, then comfort the wounded and bury the dead. I must try to wrestle the steering wheel out of the hands of the driver (2017).

Soldiers are trained to follow orders, not question them. But wars sometimes create situations in which orders should be disobeyed. The darkest day of the Vietnam War occurred when American soldiers, following orders, killed approximately 500 unarmed civilians at My Lai. Twenty-three years earlier the decision to deploy atomic bombs on Hiroshima and Nagasaki violated the principle of minimization of civilian casualties in warfare. If the soldiers at My Lai should have refused to follow their orders should the crews of the planes that delivered the atomic bombs have refused their missions as well? There are those who believe they should have refused. And there are others who believe the My Lai Massacre was unconscionable but consider the atomic bombings justifiable.

Joseph Fletcher's controversial and influential book, *Situational Ethics*, posits that laws exist for the benefit of people and should never prevent or inhibit the most loving action (1966). He viewed laws as things and insisted, "We ought to love people and use things; the essence of immorality is to love things and use people" (2014). A striking example of situational ethics is found in John Steinbeck's classic novel *Of Mice and Men*. Under normal circumstances the thought of shooting an unarmed man is reprehensible. However, the story ends with George shooting Lenny, a mentally retarded gentle giant. Lenny, literally not knowing his own strength, unintentionally killed a woman. Rather than having Lenny face the cruelty of the posse closing in on him and either life imprisonment or execution, George shoots Lenny as an act of compassion.

Fletcher's principle of the most loving action is appealing in many situations, including the termination of suffering by euthanasia. However, even in such cases determining what would constitute the most loving action can be highly subjective. Many years ago Dr. Max Schur, contrary to the Hippocratic Oath, administered a lethal dose of morphine to an elderly, cancer-ridden patient. The patient was Sigmund Freud, who had asked Schur to promise, "when the time comes, you won't let them torment me unnecessarily" (Gay, 1989, pp. 642-643). No doubt Fletcher would have approved of Dr. Schur's decision. Nevertheless, euthanasia continues to be a controversial medical ethical issue. Only three states (Oregon, Vermont, and Washington) have legalized physician-assisted suicide and 39 states have specifically legislated its prohibition.

In 1920 the renown attorney Clarence Darrow debated Frederick Starr, an anthropologist, on the question, "Is the human race getting anywhere?" In the debate Darrow said assiduous rule observation is not a human characteristic:

> Man does not live by rules. If he did, he would not live. He lives by his emotions, his instincts, his feelings; he lives as he goes along. Man does not make rules of life and then live according to those rules; he lives and then makes rules of life (1920).

Although an overstatement, he was correct in his observation that rules and emotions often are in conflict. By drawing attention to this conflict Darrow showed his agreement with Jesus that there are times when emotions, instincts, and feelings should overrule the law. Fletcher's principle of the most loving action is too subjective to be the decisive factor in all situations of conflict between rules and emotions. However, it does apply in the narrative in which Jesus declared, "The Sabbath was made for man, not man for the Sabbath" (Mark 2: 27).

Many people live according to rules they never question. They remain untroubled by their rigidity until a situation arises in which the rule not only fails to facilitate life but diminishes its quality or contributes to an injustice. Consider the implications of unfailing adherence to *always* telling the truth because telling a lie is *always* morally wrong. Great thinkers have disagreed on the immorality of lying. Immanuel Kant reasoned the truth must always be told, regardless of the consequences. Friedrich Nietzsche believed the complexities of life are such that life cannot be managed without, at least, an occasional lie. It does not require an exceptional imagination to conceptualize situations in which lying would serve a greater good.

Concerning the Sabbath observation, although a commandment Jesus taught that keeping the Sabbath should yield to "doing good" and "saving life." Acting to save a life on the Sabbath is undisputedly the right moral action. A doctor performing emergency surgery or lifeguard averting a drowning on the Sabbath is not in jeopardy of incurring God's disapproval. Deeds that are sufficiently good to suspend Sabbath observation are not always obvious. Similarly, determining "the greater good" or "the most loving act" are difficult issues frequently encountered in counseling. Jesus showed that even one of the ten commandments can be subordinated to an immediate need. Often such a determination is not easily accomplished, and in counseling judicious rule-breaking should be considered a possibility.

V. A Prophet without Honor (Mark 6: 1-6) The Rogers Principle

A family is a bunch of people who keep confusing you with someone you were as a kid.

- Robert Brault

1 Jesus left there (the region of the Gerasenes) and went to his hometown, accompanied by his disciples.
2 When the Sabbath came, he began to teach in the synagogue, and many who heard him were amazed.
"Where did this man get these things?" they asked. "What's this wisdom that has been given him, that he even does miracles!
3 Isn't this the carpenter? Isn't this Mary's son and the brother of James, Joseph, Judas and Simon? Aren't his sisters here with us?" And they took offense at him.
4 Jesus said to them, "Only in his hometown, among his relatives and in his own house is a prophet without honor."
5 He could not do any miracles there, except lay his hands on a few sick people and heal them.
6 And he was amazed at their lack of faith. Then Jesus went around teaching from village to village (Mark 6: 1-6).

Edwin Meese, Attorney General in the Reagan administration, defined an expert as "someone who is more than 50 miles from home" (2017). When Jesus returned to his hometown of Nazareth he met with resistance because he was familiar to the people there. The playwright George Bernard Shaw reflected on the human tendency to see people as they have known them in the past and wrote, "The only man who behaves sensibly is my tailor; he takes my measure anew every time he sees me, whilst all the rest go on with their old measurements, and expect them to fit me" (Malikow, 2014, p. 31).

E. Fuller Torrey, referred to in the first chapter, posited the efficacy of psychotherapy depends on four conditions, one of which is client expectations.

> There is now abundant evidence from many sources that shows the importance of expectations. What a person expects to happen often will happen if the expectations are strong enough. This is the self-fulfilling prophecy (1986, p. 55).

Those who heard Jesus teach in the synagogue were amazed at his wisdom. Jesus, in turn, was amazed at their lack of faith. In spite of his spellbinding teaching and miracles those who knew him from his childhood refused to believe that one among them could be a prophet of God. Because of their low expectations Jesus was unable to accomplish among them what he had intended. The narrative ends with him leaving Nazareth and traveling from village to village.

Expectations can be high or low depending on several factors, one of which is the overall character as seen or judged by people in general. Torrey has written, "The ability to engender hope in a client and raise expectations of being cured ultimately depends upon a therapist's reputation" (p. 63). The people of Nazareth regarded Jesus as a mere carpenter and expected nothing more than a tradesman could provide. Dr. Scott Peck, perhaps America's best known psychiatrist in the 1980's and 90's, lost credibility with many people because of a confession he made that tarnished his reputation. Several years after writing a bestselling book extolling the benefits of self-discipline he wrote another book in which he confessed to three chronic behaviors he was unsuccessful in changing. He admitted to excessive drinking, addiction to smoking, and serial adultery. Concerning his infidelity, he wrote:

> My sexual infidelity is a glaring example of the unreasonableness of romance. I would never have been diagnosed as a full-blown "sex addict," but in some ways it surely was a compulsion. ... I always wished I could have been a different kind of person who did not need such an outlet (1995, pp. 28 - 30).

Predictably, he lost the confidence of many people with whom he had credibility prior to his confession. They reasoned, if he could not help himself with the advice he offered others why should anyone expect help from him?

In addition to expectations, emotions have an influence on therapy and counseling. For this reason it is unethical for a mental health professional to have more than one relationship with a patient or client. The prohibition of "dual relationships" forbids therapists and counselors to engage in a nonprofessional relationship with anyone in their care. Treating a family member or personal friend or pursuing a romantic or business relationship with a patient or client are unconditionally unacceptable. Emotions emanating from an extraneous relationship will compromise, if not sabotage, the work to be accomplished.

An emotional distraction can arise unintentionally and unexpectedly. Several years ago I had a consultation with a young woman to discuss the possibility of therapy. Five minutes into our first and only session she suddenly arose from her chair, went to the door, and said, "I have to leave right now."

I responded, "Of course, you're free to go if you feel you must leave." I also asked her, "Before you go would you tell me why you have to leave?"

With her hand on the doorknob she said, "Last year I was raped, this is why I came here. But you look like the man who raped me. He's in prison now, but you look too much like him for me to be in a room with you."

I assured her that I understood and referred her to another therapist, a woman.

It is important for a therapist to know when not to work with someone. In addition to not engaging in a dual relationship or trying to overcome an emotional barrier, it also means not continuing to work with someone who is resistant to treatment and has no expectation of progress.

Sources of wisdom are many and diverse. "The Gambler," a country song recorded by Kenny Rogers, offers advice for playing cards that applies to life in general:

You've got to know when to hold 'em,

Know when to fold 'em,
Know when to walk away,
And know when to run (Schlitz, 1976).

The principle of withdrawing and moving on when an insurmountable problem or unalterable hindrance is encountered is part of responsible practice. To discontinue with a patient or client when ineffectiveness is unavoidable requires humility and subordination of ego to the best interest of the patient or client. Jesus knew "when to walk away."

VI. Who is the Greatest? (Mark 9: 33-37) The Trueblood Principle

He who is not a good servant will not be a good master.

- Plato

33. They (the disciples and Jesus) came to Capernaum. When he was in the house he asked them, "What were you arguing about on the road?"
34. But they kept quiet because on the way they had argued about who was the greatest.
35. Sitting down, Jesus called the Twelve and said, "If anyone wants to be first, he must be the very last, and the servant of all."
36. He took a little child and had him stand among them. Taking him in his arms he said to them,
37. "Whoever welcomes one of these little children in my name welcomes me; and whoever welcomes me does not welcome me but the one who sent me" (Mark 9: 33-37).

In this encounter with his disciples Jesus addressed their hubris. Pride is the first of the seven deadly sins and it seems odd that inflated self-estimation would be a characteristic of any of the Twelve. How could anyone mentored by Jesus be prideful and argue for his own greatness? Moreover, how could any of them take pride in having chosen to follow Jesus since he had specifically told them, "You did not choose me, but I chose you ..." (John 15:16)? A derisive statement applied to George W. Bush, Donald Trump, and others born into families of privilege is, "He was born on third base and he thinks he hit a triple." To have been chosen by Jesus is to have been born on third base.

Making a case for being the greatest required a criterion. On what basis did each disciple make his argument? The Greek word *megas* in this narrative means great in stature, rank or order. Since Simon and Andrew were the first two disciples called they would have been the greatest in seniority. But there could be no dispute on this point. Perhaps they argued over who had sacrificed the most to follow Jesus or in whom Jesus placed the most trust. Actually, it does not matter how each of them made his case. Their focus was on their greatness rather than where it should have been.

Jesus summoned a little child to serve as an object lesson and presented a paradox: "If anyone wants to be first, he must be the very last, and the servant of all" (Mark 9:35). This instruction was contrary to what they expected or even considered. It consisted of the enigmatic idea that the *greatest* must be the *least*. Jesus responded to their egoism by giving them a lesson in altruism, informing them that greatness resides in serving rather than being served. On another occasion he taught the service that honors and pleases him is that which benefits the least of people, not the greatest:

> "For I was hungry and you gave me something to eat. I was thirsty and you gave me something to drink. I was a stranger and you invited me in. I needed clothes and you clothed me. I was sick and you looked after me. I was in prison and you came to visit me." ...

"Lord, when did we see you hungry and feed you, or thirsty and give you something to drink? When did we see you a stranger and invite you in, or needing clothes and clothe you? When did we see you sick or in prison and go to visit you?" ...

"I tell you the truth, whatever you did for the least of these brothers of mine, you did for me" (Matthew 25: 35-40).

The philosopher and theologian David Elton Trueblood understood the superiority of altruism to egoism and wrote:

Man is so made that he cannot find genuine satisfaction unless his life is transcendent in at least two ways. It must transcend his own ego in that he cares more for a cause than for his own existence, and it must transcend his own brief time in that he builds for the time when he is gone and thereby denies mortality. A man has made at least a start on discovering the meaning of human life when he plants shade trees under which he knows full well he will never sit (1951, pp. 57-58).

Rabbi Harold Kushner expressed a similar thought when he wrote of the two worlds he inhabits. One is the world that recognizes him for his accomplishments and success. The other is the world that challenges him to set aside his own interests and help others. As he aged and accumulated wisdom, he found the second world of service to be the more attractive.

VI. Who is the Greatest? (Mark 9: 33-37)

As my life increasingly became a story of giving up dreams and coming to terms with my limitations ... I found myself returning more and more to that second, alternative world. I would often recall the words of my teacher, Abraham Joshua Heschel: "When I was young I admired clever people. As I grew old I came to admire kind people."

Looking back at my life, I realize that I was commuting between those two worlds in an effort to meet two basic human needs, the need to feel successful and important and the need to think of myself as a good person, someone who deserved the approval of other good people (p. 5).

The Natural, a novel written by Bernard Malamud, is the story of an extraordinarily gifted baseball player named Roy Hobbs. When asked about his drive to excel he said that his goal is to walk down the street and have those who recognize him say, "There goes Roy Hobbs, the best there ever was in the game" (1952, p. 27). While his ambition might appear admirable, he is like the disciples in that he is focused on his greatness. Another baseball novel, *Shoeless Joe*, also features another remarkably talented baseball player, Joe Jackson. In the movie version of the book Joe explains his motivation to play with these words: "God, I love this game, I would have played for meal money" (1989). In contrast to Roy, Joe is unconcerned with what people might think of him. Instead, he is driven by his sheer passion for the game.

Greatness is like happiness in that the more vigorously it is pursued the less likely it will be attained. Greatness and happiness are byproducts of other pursuits. Expressed as a simile, they are like sawdust, the byproduct of sawing wood. The disciples were vigorously arguing for their greatness rather than seeking opportunities to serve. However they perceived greatness, Jesus redefined it for them in such a way that it was actually a possibility for each of them.

Psychotherapy and counseling often manifest as directing patients and clients away from egoism and toward altruism. For the patient or client who is like Roy Hobbs and driven by a desire for accolades, it is appropriate to ask why recognition is so important. An accompanying question would be, "Are you willing to sacrifice prestige for contentment?"

There is nothing unwise or unhealthy about carefully reasoned self-interest. But self-interest to an extreme is narcissism, which is neither wise nor healthy. Trueblood understood this and wrote:

> The problem of every man is how he will sell his life and, if he is wise, he will sell it high. ... The best life is one in which, committed to some cause that has won our full loyalty, we give ourselves and all our energies to it in uncalculating and unmercenary devotion. Such lives have actually been lived, and, when we see them, we know that they are good (1951, p. 164).

VII. Repent or Perish (Luke 13: 1-5) The Chance Principle

God's love has to transcend his just retribution.
- Thornton Wilder

Everything should be made as simple as possible, but not simpler.
- Albert Einstein

1 Now there were some present at that time who told Jesus about the Galileans whose blood Pilate had mixed with their sacrifices.
2 Jesus answered, "Do you think that these Galileans were worse sinners than all the other Galileans because they suffered in this way?
3 I tell you, no! But unless you repent, you too will all perish.
4 Or those eighteen who died when the tower in Siloam fell on them - do you think they were more guilty than all the others living in Jerusalem?
5 I tell you, no! But unless you repent, you too will all perish" (Luke 13: 1-5).

The *principle of Ockham's razor*, also known as the *principle of parsimony*, teaches that explanations should be as uncomplicated as possible. While this is a good starting point for explaining an event, the simplest explanation is not always the correct one. The group Jesus addressed had an uncomplicated, but incorrect, explanation for two tragic events. One occurred when people offering sacrifices were slain at the order of Pontius Pilate, the Governor of Judea. The other occurred when a tower collapsed resulting in 18 deaths. Jesus challenged their simplistic explanation for these events. They erroneously believed the victims were singled out by God because of their egregiously sinful lives. In addition, he directed their attention to their own sinfulness, knowing they had taken comfort in the belief that their sinfulness was not as flagrant as the sinfulness of these victims.

The law of cause-and-effect asserts the irrefutable premise that every event has an antecedent. This is basis for Thornton Wilder's classic novel, *The Bridge of San Luis Rey*, in which five people plummet to their deaths when a rope bridge collapses. Upon hearing of this tragedy, a friar, Brother Juniper, makes an exhaustive attempt to understand why these five people were singled out for death. He wondered what they had in common or what in the life of each of them accounted for an untimely death. His five-year investigation resulted in no explanation. Those who told Jesus about the Galileans slain by Pilate believed a cause-and-effect relationship between gross sinfulness and calamity accounted for this tragedy. They believed the same about the 18 killed when the tower of Siloam collapsed. Like Eliphaz, one of Job's so-called comforters, they simplistically believed bad things happen only to bad people:

> Consider now: Who being innocent, has ever perished? Where were the upright ever destroyed? As I have observed, those who plow evil and those who sow trouble reap it. At the breath of God they are

destroyed; at the blast of his anger they perish (Job 4: 7-9).

Such reasoning disregards the unfortunate reality that bad things happen to good people just as good things happen to bad people. Job's story is not that of a sinful man getting his just punishment. To the contrary, in a conversation with Satan the Lord singled out Job as a righteous man:

> ... the Lord said to Satan, "Have you considered my servant Job? There is no one on earth like him; he is blameless and upright, a man who fears God and shuns evil" (1:8).

Nevertheless, Job suffers the loss of his children, wealth, physical health, and good standing in the community.

Conversely, the Psalmist was puzzled by the good fortune of the wicked:

> They have no struggles; their bodies are healthy and strong. They are free from the burdens common to man; they are not plagued by human ills (Psalm 73: 4-5).

Admittedly, this observation is hyperbolic. In a more measured statement, Paul, writing to the Galatians, warns that evildoers are not exempt from the consequences of their behavior.

Do not be deceived; God cannot be mocked. A man reaps what he sows. The one who sows to please his sinful nature, from that nature will reap destruction; the one who sows to please the Spirit, from the Spirit will reap eternal life (Galatians 6:7,8).

Although Paul was addressing ultimate judgment, the concept of the *law of the harvest* applies to earthly life as well. Experience teaches that everyday choices have immediate as well as ripple effects, giving significance to decisions that seem mundane.

The parable Jesus proceeded to tell his inquirers provided a correction to their thinking:

A man had a fig tree planted in his vineyard, and he went to look for fruit on it, but did not find any. So he said to the man who took care of the vineyard, "For three years now I've been coming to look for fruit on this fig tree and haven't found any. Cut it down! Why should it use up the soil?"

"Sir," the man replied, "leave it alone for one more year, and I'll dig around it and fertilize it. If it bears fruit next year, fine! If not, then cut it down" (Luke 13: 6-9).

In this parable God is the man caring for the vineyard, not the owner. The owner's patience with the unproductive fig tree has been exhausted. The caretaker appeals for more time to nurture this tree that is only using up the soil. This is a parable of grace, conveying an alternative view to that of an angry God who used Pilate and a tower as instruments for punishment. Through this parable Jesus conveyed, "Your understanding of God is too narrow; He is also long-suffering with sinners, including all of you." The parable ends with the caretaker saying if a year of special attention does not result in fruit then the tree will be cut down. This ending teaches that sinners do not have unlimited time for repentance, God's graciousness notwithstanding.

In commenting on these two tragedies Jesus addressed another of his listeners' misunderstandings. Twice he said to them, "But unless you repent, you too will all perish" (Luke 13: 3,5). With these words he warned them of their complacency, which had arisen from their belief that they were not sinners of the worst order since they did not perish in either of these events. Their estimation of their standing before God was based on two misunderstandings. One, that a tragic death is proof positive of an especially sinful life. Two, God evaluates righteousness by comparing one person with another. Concerning such a comparison, imagine a criminal trial in which the defense of the accused is, "Not guilty, because other people have done much worse." The "Riddle of the Coal Miners" teaches that accurate self-estimation cannot be acquired by looking at another person:

> Two coal miners emerge from a coal mine at the end of the workday, look at each other, say "goodbye," and go to their respective homes for dinner. One of the miners has a clean face, the face of the other is

blackened from coal soot. Oddly, the man with the clean face washes his face before sitting down for dinner and the man with the dirty face sits for dinner without washing. Why?

The answer is the man with the clean face looked at the man with the dirty face and assumed his face must be dirty as well since they came from the same place. The man with the dirty face looked at the man clean face and assumed his face must also be clean since they both emerged from the mine. The point of this riddle is looking at another person is not the way to arrive at an accurate self-understanding.

Psychotherapy and counseling often involve challenging a misconception, suggesting an expanded view, and/or redirecting patients and clients away from others and toward themselves. Aaron Beck, the father of *cognitive behavioral therapy* referred to in chapter II, understood this. Two of the features of this approach to therapy are *cognitive restructuring* and challenging the patient's indefensible and/or illogical conclusions.

Cognitive restructuring occurs when the therapist encourages patients to reconsider the facts of their situation and entertain equally reasonable alternative interpretations. The parable of the unproductive fig tree did not alter the facts of the two tragedies. Instead, it presented a view of God as nurturing and patient rather than judgmental and punishing.

The conclusion that the worst sinners in Jerusalem were killed by Pilate's order and the tower's collapse was not the only possible explanation for these occurrences. It was and is also possible that God allows things to happen for reasons beyond human comprehension. The prophet Jeremiah asked God, "Why does the way of the wicked prosper? Why do all the faithless live at ease?" (Jeremiah 12:1). He was not given the answer because he would not have been able to fathom it. God's response might have seemed enigmatic to Jeremiah: "If you have raced with men on foot and they have worn you out, how can you compete with horses?" (12: 5). This was God's way of saying to Jeremiah that he would win a foot race with a horse before he would ever comprehend why some conditions exist.

Humility is required to concede that many of God's ways exceed human understanding. Job was never given the reason for his ineffable suffering. Unlike Jeremiah and Job, the people Jesus encountered preferred a wrong explanation to no explanation. This in spite of the word of God through the prophet Isaiah:

> For my thoughts are not your thoughts, neither are your ways my ways. As the heavens are higher than the earth, so are my ways higher than your ways and my thoughts than your thoughts (Isaiah 55: 8,9).

The Psalmist speculated if divine punishment was administered in proportion to sin then no one would be alive: "If you, O Lord, kept a record of sins, O Lord, who could stand?" (Psalm 130: 3).

VII. Repent or Perish (Luke 13: 1-5)

In addition to cognitive restructuring, psychotherapy and counseling often involve directing patients and clients away from the sins and failures of others and toward their own shortcomings. Sue Chance, a psychiatrist, cautions against using therapy to focus on the faults of others:

> I do not like my parents and I do not like the things they did to me. However, I am responsible for who I am now. There is no way I can reasonably say that, at forty-nine, I am more a product of the first fifteen years I spent with them than I am of the past thirty-four years I have spent with myself. I would, in fact, be very ashamed of myself if it were true (1992, pp. 146-147).

Her advice to many of her patients is,

> ... you're getting closer and closer to the time in your life when you can take over and make it better for yourself. That's going to be your choice: whether you stay stuck in blaming and moaning about all the things that have been unfair or get on with it and do the best you can with what you have (p. 146).

Psychotherapy that is merely a venue for comparisons with and complaints about other people is psychotherapy that is failing the patient. In contrast, if it is instrumental in helping patients entertain other perspectives and new ideas while focusing on themselves then they are being well-served.

VIII. Crucified with Two Criminals (Luke 23: 32, 39-43) The Selzer Principle

No one is useless in this world who lightens the burdens of another.

- Charles Dickens

32 Two other men, both criminals, were also led out with him to be executed.
39. One of the criminals who hung there hurled insults at him: "Aren't you the Messiah? Save yourself and us!"
40. But the other criminal rebuked him. "Don't you fear God," he said, "since you are under the same sentence?
41. We are punished justly, for we are getting what our deeds deserve. But this man has done nothing wrong."
42. Then he said, "Jesus, remember me when you come into your kingdom."
43. Jesus answered him, "Truly I tell you, today you will be with me in paradise" (Luke 23: 32, 39-43).

The gospels record seven statements made by Jesus when he was being crucified. Three of them show concern for others in the midst of his own suffering:

> "Father forgive them; for they do not know what they are doing." (Luke 23: 34)

> "Dear woman, here is your son. Here is your mother." (John 19: 26)

VIII. Crucified with Two Criminals (Luke 23: 32, 39-43)

"Truly I tell you, today you will be with me in paradise." (Luke 23: 43).

The question of whether Jesus asked the Father to forgive all of humanity, all those associated with his death or only the Roman soldiers who were carrying out his execution has been a matter of debate among New Testament scholars. What is not debatable is Jesus' intercession on behalf of others in the waning moments of his life. Jesus' concern for his mother's well-being after his death was expressed by directing Mary to look to John, the disciple whom he loved, for the care Jesus had provided. The repentant criminal received Jesus' reassurance that they would be together in paradise that very day. The consideration Jesus showed the repentant criminal is the focus of this chapter.

Excruciating, a word used to describe extreme pain, literally means "from the cross" (*ex crucio* in Latin). Who would fault Jesus for being preoccupied with his own suffering? Yet, he heard the pain, terror, and repentance in the voice of another and responded with compassion. Jesus gave comfort when he himself needed it most.

Kay Jamison's memoir, *An Unquiet Mind*, begins with her recollection of someone who cared for others in the midst of his own life-threatening situation. She remembered a jet pilot who sacrificed his life for the safety of others:

The noise of the jet had become louder, and I saw the children in my second-grade class suddenly dart their heads upward. The plane was coming in very low, and then it streaked past us, scarcely missing the playground. As we stood there clumped together and absolutely terrified, it flew into the trees and exploded directly in front of us. ...Over the next few days it became clear, from the release of the young pilot's final message to the control tower before he died, that he knew he could save his own life by bailing out. He also knew, however, that by doing so he risked that his unaccompanied plane would fall onto the playground and kill those of us who were there (Jamison, 1995, pp. 12-13).

A therapist should never be defensive, indignant, retaliatory, autobiographical, haughty or condescending. Expressed as colloquial phrase, "It's never about you." Patients and clients are never well-served by a therapist or counselor who is self-interested or, even worse, self-absorbed. Richard Selzer, a surgeon and author, confessed to an incident that occurred early in his career when he retaliated against an uncooperative, verbally abusive patient. Selzer, working in an emergency room, was exhausted after many hours without sleep. The patient refused to lie still and allow Selzer to suture a deep cut across the forehead. Exasperated, he took action against the patient, who was lying on the examining table restrained by straps around his arms. With a grin, Selzer informed him, "I have sewn your ears to the stretcher, move and you'll rip them off" (1982, p. 61). Although he was able to complete his work, 25 years later Dr. Selzer wrote:

VIII. Crucified with Two Criminals (Luke 23: 32, 39-43)

Even now, so many years later, this ancient rage of mine returns to peck among my dreams. I have only to close my eyes and see him wielding his head and jaws, to hear once more those words at which the of whole trussed body came hurtling toward me. How sorry I will always be. Not being able to make it up to him for that grin (p. 63).

To his credit, Selzer remained haunted by the time when he failed to divest himself of self-interest and turned his anger upon his patient. Jesus met the challenge that confronts every therapist and counselor - the challenge to lay aside self and serve another without compromise.

IX. Jesus Talks with a Samaritan Woman (John 4: 1-26) The Livingston Principle

Being entirely honest with oneself is a good exercise.
- Sigmund Freud

1 The Pharisees heard that Jesus was gaining and baptizing more disciples than John,

2 although in fact it was not Jesus who baptized, but his disciples.

3 When the Lord learned of this, he left Judea and went once more to Galilee.

4 Now he had to go through Samaria.

5 So he came to a town in Samaria called Sychar, near the plot of ground Jacob had given to his son Joseph.

6 Jacob's well was there, and Jesus, tired as he was from the journey, sat down by the well. It was about noon.

7 When a Samaritan woman came to draw water, Jesus said to her, "Will you give me a drink?"

8 (His disciples had gone into the town to buy food.)

9 The Samaritan woman said to him, "You are a Jew and I am a Samaritan woman. How can you ask me for a drink?" (For Jews do not associate with Samaritans.)

10 Jesus answered her, "If you knew the gift of God and who it is that asks you for a drink, you would have asked him and he would have given you living water."

11 "Sir," the woman said, "you have nothing to draw with and the well is deep. Where can you get this living water?

12 Are you greater than our father Jacob, who gave us the well and drank from it himself, as did also his sons and his livestock?"

IX. Jesus Talks with a Samaritan Woman (John 4: 1-26)

13 Jesus answered, "Everyone who drinks this water will be thirsty again,

14 but whoever drinks the water I give him will never thirst. Indeed, the water I give him will become in him a spring of water welling up to eternal life."

15 The woman said to him, "Sir, give me this water so that I won't get thirsty and have to keep coming here to draw water."

16 He told her, "Go, call your husband and come back."

17 "I have no husband," she replied. Jesus said to her, "You are right when you say you have no husband.

18 The fact is, you have had five husbands, and the man you now have is not your husband. What you have just said is quite true."

19 "Sir," the woman said, "I can see that you are a prophet.

20 Our ancestors worshiped on this mountain, but you Jews claim that the place where we must worship is in Jerusalem."

21 "Woman," Jesus replied, "believe me, a time is coming when you will worship the Father neither on this mountain nor in Jerusalem.

22 You Samaritans worship what you do not know; we worship what we do know, for salvation is from the Jews.

23 Yet a time is coming and has now come when the true worshipers will worship the Father in spirit and truth, for they are the kind of worshipers the Father seeks.

24 God is spirit, and his worshipers must worship in spirit and in truth."

25 The woman said, "I know that Messiah" (called Christ) "is coming. When he comes, he will explain everything to us."

26 Then Jesus declared, "I, the one speaking to you—I am he" (John 4: 1-26).

The antagonism between Jews and Samaritans had a long history. The Jews considered the Samaritans an inferior class of Jewish people, if they were considered Jews at all. The intensity of this division was such that the Samaritans maintained their own house of worship on Mount Gerizim while the Jews worshipped at the Temple in Jerusalem. One scholar has characterized this rift in contemporary terms:

> Imagine the hatred between Serbs and Muslims in modern Bosnia, the enmity between Catholics and Protestants in Northern Ireland or the feuding between street gangs in Los Angeles or New York, and you have some idea of the feeling and its causes between Jews and Samaritans in the time of Jesus (McCloskey, 2017).

The Samaritan woman recognized Jesus as a Jew and was surprised that he would even speak to her. After a double entendre discussion about water Jesus told her to summon her husband. She responded honestly, saying, "I have no husband." Jesus then amazed her by accurately commenting on her marital past, moving her to declare him a prophet. But rather than continuing a conversation about her personal life she tried to change the subject. By raising an issue concerning religious practice she hoped to distract the prophet away from her multiple marriages and current situation.

But Jesus would have none of that. Although a rabbi, in this encounter he was not interested in a discussion about law or custom. Rather, his interest was in this woman with an extraordinary marital history. Jesus seized upon her observation about the two locations for worship as a segue to addressing her relationship with God. He told her the worship that pleases God is not a geographical issue but a matter of the heart. A flippant, contemporary way of expressing this idea is, *merely sitting in church on Sunday doesn't make a person a Christian any more than sitting in a parking lot makes a person a car.*

By trying to initiate a discussion about the proper location for worship she was employing the defense mechanism of *intellectualization.* In Freudian psychoanalytic theory people are defensive when they experience anxiety because of something they know to be true at the unconscious level. Intellectualization is the defense mechanism by which an individual, detached from feelings, can pursue an emotionally disturbing topic as an idea. Having recognized Jesus as a prophet, she unconsciously wanted to discuss her relationship with God. But her multiple marriages and, probably, other features of her life made this discussion threatening. So she proposed an academic discussion of right relationship with God by making it a conversation about where to worship. If she could remove herself as the subject she would be able to impersonally discuss how right relationship with God is attained.

A quotation attributed to Sir Winston Churchill is, "If we spend too much of the present talking about the past we will have no future." While endless ruminations about the past rarely produce a benefit, some examination of the past is necessary to understand the present and plan for the future. Psychotherapy requires visiting the patient's past without establishing a residence there. It is understandable when a patient does not want to visit a past that includes painful events and regrettable behaviors. Intellectualization is one way of avoiding a review that will be unpleasant, if not humiliating. It can take the form of patients using psychological jargon to express themselves impersonally. A patient might say, "I am experiencing ego dystonic behavior" instead of, "I hate myself because of the selfish and cruel things I do to the people I love." Such a patient should be told, "Your task is to express yourself in your own words, not the words you've read in a psychology textbook."

As previously stated, intellectualization can also take the form of abstract discussion. Imagine a suicidal patient who wants to talk about suicide, but in an impersonal way. Such a patient might address the subject obliquely by raising questions about the meaning of life and the inevitability of death. Gordon Livingston, a psychiatrist, does not discuss suicide as a philosophical issue with his patients:

> When confronted with a suicidal person I seldom try to talk them out of it. Instead I ask them to examine what it is that so far has dissuaded them from killing themselves. Usually this involves finding out what the connections are that tether that person to life in the face of nearly unbearable psychic pain (2004, p. 72).

He also confronts his suicidal patients with their selfishness:

> People in despair are, naturally, intensely self-absorbed. Suicide is the ultimate expression of this preoccupation with self. Instead of just expressing sympathy and fear that suicidal people evoke in those around them, therapists included, I think it is reasonable to confront them with the selfishness and anger implied in any act of self-destruction (p. 72).

Dr. Livingston engages these patients in a discussion of their own life and unique set of circumstances. He does not pursue an exploration of suicide as a philosophical issue for humankind but an existential reality for his patient. Like Jesus with the Samaritan woman, Dr. Livingston does not allow his patients to divert his attention from his work by enticing him with debatable abstractions.

X. Progressive Disclosure (John 16: 1-4, 12) The Saunders Principle

When the student is ready the teacher arrives.

- Anonymous

1 "All this I have told you so that you will not go astray.
2 They will put you out of the synagogue; in fact, a time is coming when anyone who kills you will think he is offering a service to God.
3 They will do such things because they have not known the Father or me.
4 I have told you this, so that when the time comes you will remember that I warned you. I did not tell this at first because I was with you. ...
12 I have much more to say, more than you can now bear" (John 16: 1-4, 12).

With his arrest, trial, and execution imminent, Jesus gathered his disciples and told them things they needed to know since he would not be with them much longer. He also told them he had other things he could tell them but these things were beyond their understanding. In this narrative Jesus is demonstrating *progressive revelation* - pacing his communication according to necessity or the disciples' readiness to understand it. Concerning necessity, there were some things the disciples did not need to know as long as Jesus was with them. Concerning readiness, there were other things the disciples were unprepared to comprehend. Telling them, "I have much more to say, more than you can now bear" is not a condescending rant like that of Jack Nicholson's character in "A Few Good Men" when he blustered, "You can't handle the truth!" (1992). Rather, it was a statement of sensitivity, showing Jesus' wisdom by not burdening the disciples with superfluous information.

Applied to psychotherapy and counseling, progressive revelation means telling patients and clients what they need to know when they need to know it or limiting communication to what they can understand in the present. Often, this makes the therapist's work developmental, preparing the patient or client for what lies ahead.

It is not unusual for patients to ask for their diagnosis, something they rarely need and are likely to misunderstand. Irvin Yalom cautions against providing one prematurely because it has a limiting effect on the therapist:

> Why? For one thing psychotherapy consists of a gradual unfolding process wherein the therapist attempts to know the patient as fully as possible. A diagnosis limits vision; it diminishes the ability to relate to the other as a person. Once we make a diagnosis we tend to selectively in attend to aspects of the patient that do not fit into that particular diagnosis, and correspondingly overattend to subtle features that appear to confirm an initial diagnosis (2003, pp. 4-5).

In addition, a diagnosis can also have a limiting effect on the patient. Patients who believe a diagnosis defines them do not appreciate the complexity of who they are. Moreover, these patients might resign themselves to a prognosis that underestimates the influence of their resolve to get well. It is not an overstatement to say that Yalom has contempt for diagnoses, except for conditions with a biological substrate. "Today's psychotherapy students are exposed to too much emphasis on diagnosis. (Diagnosis) has precious little to do with reality. It represents instead an illusory attempt to legislate scientific precision into being when it is neither possible nor desirable" (p. 4).

Progressive revelation is an important part of *The Chosen*, a novel written by Chaim Potok. Set in post-World War II Brooklyn, it is the story of the friendship of two very different Jewish boys. Daniel Saunders is part of a devoutly religious community steeped in tradition, the Hasidim. Reuven Malter, is a non-religious Zionist, fiercely devoted to the creation of Israel as a homeland for the Jewish people. Early in their friendship Reuven learns that Daniel has been raised in silence by his father, the rabbi of the Hasidic community. This means Daniel and his father speak to each other only when they are studying the Torah, the Jewish law. Reuven is amazed by what he perceives as Rabbi Saunders' unspeakable cruelty.

Near the story's end Rabbi Saunders, in Daniel's presence, explains to Reuven why Daniel was raised in silence. At an early age Daniel demonstrated stunning genius by reading well before expected and remembering verbatim all that he had read. To his father's dismay, with Daniel's brilliance came an attitude of superiority and insensitivity toward others. It was then that Rabbi Saunders determined he would raise Daniel in silence. Hurt and confused by his father's withdrawal, Daniel eventually came to appreciate and understand the pain of others and grew to be an exceptionally patient, kind, and sensitive young man.

Rabbi Saunders' explanation could not have come earlier. Being perplexed by his father's detachment was necessary for the development of Daniel's empathy. When his father could see that his parenting strategy had succeeded he revealed to Daniel the reason for it. Daniel was told what he needed to know when he needed to know it and when he could understand it.

Progressive revelation is a foundational teaching of the Baha'i faith. Its founder, Baha'u'llah, used the metaphor of a robe to characterize wisdom and justice:

> Whenever this robe hath fulfilled its purpose, the Almighty will assuredly renew it. For every age requireth a fresh measure of the light of God. Every Divine Revelation hath been sent down in a manner that befitted the circumstances of the age in which it hath appeared (1990, p. 81).

Similarly, Yalom has written,

> Even if the therapist does not make full and explicit interpretations about the unconscious roots of a patient's problems, the therapist may still, with subtlety and good timing, make comments that, at a deep

unspoken level, "click" with the patient's unconscious and allow the latter to feel completely understood (1980, pp. 190-191).

XI. Jesus before Pilate (John 18: 33-40)
The Sartre Principle

In the end, we are answerable for the kind of persons we have made of ourselves.

- William Bennett

33 Pilate then went back inside the palace, summoned Jesus and asked him, "Are you the king of the Jews?"
34 "Is that your idea," Jesus asked, "or did others talk to you about me?"
35 "Am I a Jew?" Pilate replied. "It was your people and your chief priests who handed you over to me. What is it you have done?"
36 Jesus said, "My kingdom is not of this world. If it were, my servants would fight to prevent my arrest by the Jews. But now my kingdom is from another place."
37 "You are a king, then!" said Pilate. Jesus answered, "You are right in saying I am a king. In fact, for this reason I was born, and for this I came into the world, to testify to the truth. Everyone on the side of truth listens to me."
38 "What is truth?" Pilate asked. With this he went out again to the Jews and said, "I find no basis for a charge against him.
39 But it is your custom for me to release to you one prisoner at the time of the Passover. Do you want me to release 'the king of the Jews'?"
40 They shouted back, "No, not him! Give us Barabbas!" ... (John 18: 33-40).

The Apostles' Creed, an early statement of Christian faith, includes the affirmation that Jesus suffered under Pontius

Pilate. Conversely, it is also accurate to state that Pilate suffered under Jesus. Pilate did not want the responsibility of judging and sentencing Jesus and made five futile attempts at evasion. He deferred to the crowd, hoping they would call for the release of Jesus rather than Barabbas (Matthew 27:21). He sent Jesus to Herod to be judged, only to have Jesus returned to him (Luke 23: 1-12). He instructed the Sanhedrin to judge Jesus according to Jewish law, but Roman law forbade the Sanhedrin to exercise the punishment their law required - execution (John 18: 28-32). He appealed to Jesus to defend himself by denying the charge against him (John 19: 6-12). He hoped a token punishment, a flogging, would satisfy those insisting on crucifixion (Luke 23: 20-25).

When Pilate asked Jesus if he was the king of the Jews, Jesus' response was a call to responsibility: "Is that your idea, or did others talk to you about me?" Jesus issued a second challenge to Pilate when he said, "Everyone on the side of truth listens to me." After rhetorically asking, "What is truth?" Pilate incriminated himself by declaring, "I find no basis for a charge against him." In the midst of all this Pilate received a message from his wife, telling him, "Don't have anything to do with that innocent man, for I have suffered a great deal today in a dream because of him" (Matthew 27: 19).

Psychiatrist and bestselling author Scott Peck has written, "Triggers are pulled by individuals. Orders are given and executed by individuals. In the last analysis, every single human act is ultimately the result of an individual choice" (1983, p. 215). Implicit in Dr. Peck's analysis is free will with consequent responsibility is a reality. While for centuries philosophers have engaged in the *free will vs. determinism* debate, authentic choice-making and ensuing responsibility are widely accepted in clinical psychology. Yalom believes free will is one of four recurring issues in psychotherapy:

> I have found that four givens are particularly relevant to psychotherapy: the inevitability of death for each of us and those we love; the freedom to make our lives as we will; our ultimate aloneness; and, finally, the absence of any obvious meaning or sense to life (1989, pp. 4-5).

Psychotherapy and counseling often take the form of a call to responsibility by challenging patients and clients to make a declaration and examine their behavior in the light of that declaration. In the above narrative Pilate twice responded to a question with a question in an effort to avoid declaring himself. When patients or clients evade a question it is my practice to tell them, "You don't have to answer any question I ask. However, it might be helpful to you if we discuss why you don't want to answer."

Pilate asked Jesus, "Are you king of the Jews?" Before affirming that he was, Jesus asked Pilate, "Is this your own idea or did others talk to you about me?" By asking this, Jesus gave Pilate an opportunity to declare that the trial would be fair and untainted by the opinions and interests of the Sanhedrin. Pilate responded with a question ("Am I a Jew?") followed by the statement that the trial was not initiated by him but by Jesus' own people. In this exchange Pilate is trying to distance himself from the responsibility for these proceedings.

According to William Bennett, by definition, responsible people assume responsibility: "To 'respond' is to 'answer.' Correspondingly, to be 'responsible' is to be 'answerable,' to be *accountable*. Irresponsible behavior is immature behavior. Taking responsibility - being responsible - is a sign of maturity" (1993, p. 185).

Psychotherapy and counseling often direct patients and clients to the discomforting truth that a "weakened *sense* of responsibility does not weaken the *fact* of responsibility" (p. 186). In *Existentialism and Human Emotions* Jean-Paul Sartre wrote,

> I say that man is condemned to be free. Condemned, because he did not create himself, yet in other respects free; because, once thrown into the world, he is responsible for everything he does (1957, p. 23).

Before ordering the release of Barabbas and the execution of Jesus, Pilate literally washed his hands in front of the crowd and said, "I am innocent of this man's blood. It is your responsibility!" (Matthew 27:24). In addition,

> Pilate had a notice prepared and had it fastened to the cross. It read: JESUS OF NAZARETH, THE KING OF THE JEWS. Many of the Jews read the sign, for the place where Jesus was crucified was near the

city, and the sign was written in Aramaic, Latin and Greek. The chief priests of the Jews protested to Pilate, "Do not write 'The King of the Jews,' but that this man claimed to be king of the Jews."

Pilate answered, "What I have written, I have written" (John 19: 19-22).

Neither of Pilate's bold statements relieved him of the responsibility for ordering the death of an innocent man. Bold statements are not to be equated with bold action. "It is a truism that everything that has ever been done in the history of the world has been done by *somebody*; some person has exercised some power to *do* it" (Bennett, 1993, p. 185). These harsh and burdensome realities are often conveyed in psychotherapy and counseling.

Epilogue: Five Views of a Good Life

The unexamined life is not worth living.

- Socrates

Compared to lawyer jokes, there are few jokes directed toward psychiatrists. One of the few takes the form of a lightbulb joke:

> Question: How many psychiatrists does it take to change a lightbulb?
> Answer: Only one, but the light bulb has to really want to change.

In a more serious vein, Jerome Frank expressed the same thought in his classic, *Persuasion and Healing*:

> A patient's willingness to admit distress, especially in conjunction with personal problems, implies a willingness to make humiliating self-revelations, which in itself is evidence that he trusts the psychiatrist and expects to be helped by him. It also implies dissatisfaction with one's self, hence motivation to change (1961, p. 137).

Psychotherapy and counseling are concerned with change, which is to say they are initiated by patients and clients who are discontent with their *status quo*. In psychotherapy the discontentment is with the self; in counseling the dissatisfaction is with the state of affairs. The former requires introspection and openness to change. The latter calls for problem solving strategies or the acceptance that some problems are insoluble. In both endeavors a better life is sought, which is part of an ongoing quest for a good life. Concerning this quest, John Whitehorn has written:

> There are many persons disturbed by unanswerable doubts, who need the reasoning hand of a wise and trusted guide. Others, jumping from the frying pan of doubt into the fire of urgent, but poorly chosen action, need both a helping hand and a pointing finger to see the situation as it is and as it may be remedied. For all persons, coping with life situations is inherently a cooperating enterprise, in which everyone, at some time or other, needs help and guidance from another (Frank, 1961, p. vii).

Work and Love

What constitutes a good life? William James characterized it as happiness when he wrote, "How to gain, how to keep, how to discover happiness is in fact, for most men at all times the secret motive for all they do" (2017). Philosophers and psychologists (James was both) characterize happiness as *overall contentment with one's life*. This is what Aristotle had in mind when he defined happiness as "an activity of the soul in accordance with virtue" (Martin, 1989, p. 40). (*Eudaimonia* is the Greek word translated as "happiness" but it is more precisely understood as "the flourishing life.")

When asked about a good life Freud is reputed to have said, *lieben und arbeiten* (work and love). Even if Freud did not say this, Leo Tolstoy did when he wrote, "One can live magnificently in this world, if one knows how to work and how to love, to work for the person one loves and to love one's work" (Troyat, 1967, p. 158). Tolstoy and, possibly, Freud believed the path to a good life consists of personally meaningful work and at least one relationship in which love is given and received.

While work and love constitute one path to a good life, there are others. But none of them offers a guaranteed route to this coveted destination. If a good life is attainable the course to it is one that integrates the wise counsel of several paths. The therapy and counseling provided by Jesus embodies the essential features of each of the following paths.

Stoicism

Stoicism is associated with Epictetus (c. 50 - 135 AD), a Greek philosopher who taught from the *Stoa Poikile* (painted porch), from which the name of this philosophy derives. In contemporary usage, the word stoic describes a person who shows no emotion, especially in an unfortunate situation. The teaching of stoicism is to approach life by placing events and situations into one of two categories: those that are subject to one's control and those that are not. In addition, attention and effort should be given only to things that are controllable and resignation to things that are not.

When Jesus said, "do not worry about tomorrow, for tomorrow will worry about itself," and added, "each day has enough trouble of its own" he conveyed a stoic principle (Matthew 6: 34). He taught his followers to focus on their current problems because those were the problems over which they might exercise some control. The same tenet is embedded in what is perhaps the best known of Jesus' parables, "The Parable of the Lost Son" (Luke 15: 11-32). In this story the wise and loving father accepted that he could not make his son want to remain at home. The father resigned himself to the painful truth that the only way his son would intrinsically desire to live at home would be to let him experience life in a distant country.

Hedonism

Hedonism derives from *hedone*, the Greek word for pleasure. Hedonists believe there are only two motivations for human behavior - pleasure and pain. They believe decision-making should be guided by calculating pleasure and pain and acting in such a way as to maximize pleasure and minimize pain. This will often manifest as estimating risk and reward.

Contrary to what many believe, hedonism does not advocate the unbridled pursuit of pleasure. Those who erroneously believe this will find it incredulous that one of Jesus' teachings has an hedonic element. The lesson described in Luke 14: 25-33 includes two illustrations of *counting the cost* of an anticipated action. One is that of a builder who began a project with insufficient funds to finish it. The other is that of a king who went off to war with too few men to engage the enemy and decided to surrender before the war began. Jesus concluded this lesson with, "In the same way, any of you who does not give up everything he has cannot be my disciple" (vs. 33). An impulsive action rarely provides a favorable result. For this reason Jesus strongly encouraged counting the cost or, as a hedonist would express it, calculating pleasure and pain.

Altruism

According to the contemporary philosopher Thomas Nagel, "Altruism depends on the recognition of the reality of other persons, and on the equivalent capacity to regard oneself as merely one individual among many" (1970, p. 3). While Jesus was being crucified he recognized the reality of his mother, those responsible for his execution, and a repentant criminal and expressed concern for each of them. The antithesis of altruism is *egoism*, the practice of placing self-interest above the interests of others. Defined in this way, egoism is incompatible with a good life. Jesus epitomized altruism at Calvary.

Mindfulness

Buddhism is the religion founded approximately 25 centuries ago by Siddhartha Guatama, a Nepali prince. Through reflection he discovered the path to liberation from suffering (*dharma*) making him the Buddha, which means "the awakened one." The foundation of Buddhism is the *Four Noble Truths*:

Life is suffering.
Suffering is the result of attachment and desire.
It is possible to end suffering.
The best life is the life of the eightfold path.

The first three truths concern suffering, but not as suffering is commonly understood. Suffering in Buddhism is the result of attachment to or desire for anything "incapable of satisfying." This includes people, experiences, and material objects. The path out of suffering is detachment from these things that cannot satisfy. This does not mean life cannot be enjoyed. *Mindfulness* means enjoying those things that are pleasurable without wishing they would never end. It is unwise to become attached to anything that is pleasant because everything is transitory. Embracing this reality and following the eightfold path (eight principles for life) will eventuate in *nirvana*, a perfect state of happiness and peace in which there is release from all forms of suffering and preoccupation with self.

Recall Jesus' encounter with the rich ruler in which Jesus directed him to sell his possessions, distribute the proceeds to the poor, and follow as a disciple (Luke 18: 18-27). Jesus gave this directive because the rich ruler was attached to his considerable material wealth and desired to retain it, even though he sensed it was incapable of satisfying him. This does not mean Jesus himself could not enjoy a pleasant occasion. His first miracle was performed at a wedding feast where he turned water into wine (John 2: 1-11). Neither does it mean he was unremittingly ascetic and insisted on the same for his disciples. When asked why his disciples did not fast he said, "How can the guests of the bridegroom mourn while he is with them? The time will come when the bridegroom will be taken from them, then they will fast" (Matthew 9:15).

Aristotle's *golden mean* is the desirable middle between two extremes, one of excess and the other of deficiency. Jesus and the Buddha taught that the pleasurable things in life can be enjoyed if they are not clutched with an unwillingness to relinquish them. A good life cannot include attachment to those things that are incapable of satisfying.

Conclusion

Daniel Robinson, Distinguished Professor of Philosophy Emeritus at Georgetown University and Oxford University Fellow, concluded his lecture "Four Theories on the Good Life" with this summary: "The good life is active, contemplative, somewhat fatalistic, and selfless" (2017). This is an excellent characterization of a good life. Jesus saw the same features in a good life and taught accordingly as well as personifying them.

References

Introduction

Haidt, J. (2006). *The happiness hypothesis: Finding modern truth in ancient wisdom.* New York: Perseus Books Group.

Shaw, G. (2017). Recovered from https://www.brainyquote.com/quotes/quotes/g/georgebern on 05/06/2017.

I. How Do Counseling and Psychotherapy Differ?

Myers, D. (2010). *Psychology (ninth edition).* New York: Worth Publishers

Torrey, E. (1986). *Witchdoctors and psychiatrists: The common roots of psychotherapy and its future.* Northvale, NJ: Jason Aronson, Inc.

II. The Rich Young Man

Nietzsche, F. (1976). *Thus spake Zarathustra: A book for all or none.* Walter Kaufmann, translator. New York: Random House.

References

Yalom, I. (2008). *Staring at the sun: Overcoming the terror of death*. San Francisco, CA: Jossey Bass.

III. Paying Taxes to Caesar

Holmes, A. (1977). *All truth is God's truth*. Grand Rapids, MI: W.B. Eerdman's Publishing Company.

IV. Lord of the Sabbath

Bonhoeffer, D. (2017). Recovered from http://www.azquotes .com on 05/22/2017.

Dalai Lama (2017). Recovered from http://1stholistic.com /reading/liv_reading-dalai-lama-instructions-for-life-millennium.htm on 05/19/2017.

Darrow, C. (1920). "Is the human race getting anywhere?" Chicago, IL: Maclaskey and Maclaskey (reporters).

Eigen, Z., Sherwyn, D., Ceriale, M., and Menillo, N. (2015). "When rules are made to be broken." *Northwestern university law review*. Vol. 109. No. 1.

Fletcher, J. (1966). *Situation ethics: The new morality*. Santa Ana, CA: Westminster Press.

_____ . (2014) Recovered from Thinkexist.com website on 05/21/2017.

Gay, C. (1989). *Freud: A life for our times*. New York: W.W. Norton Company.

King, M.L. (1989). "Letter from Birmingham jail." *Ethics in America: Source reader.* Newton, L.H., editor. Englewood Cliffs, NJ: Prentice Hall.

V. A Prophet without Honor

Torrey, E. (1986). *Witchdoctors and psychiatrists: The common roots of psychiatry and its future.* Northvale, NJ: Jason Aronson Inc.

Malikow, M. (2014). *It's not too late! Making the most of the rest of your life.* (Third edition). Chipley, FL: Theocentric Publishing.

Meese, E. (2017). Recovered from https://www.brainyquote .com/search_results. Html?q=edwin+meese on 05/26/ 2017.

Peck, S. (1995). *In search of stones*. New York: Hyperion Books.

Schlitz, D. (1976). "The gambler." Beverly Hills, CA: United Artists.

VI. Who Is the Greatest?

"Field of Dreams." (1989). Universal City Studios. MCA Universal Home Video.

Kushner, H. (2001). *Living a life that matters*. New York: Anchor Books.

Malamud, B. (1952). *The natural*. New York: Farrar, Strauss, and Cudahy.

Trueblood, D. (1951). *The life we prize*. New York: Harper & Brothers Publishers.

VII. Repent or Perish

Chance, S. (1992). *Stronger than death: When suicide touches your life*. New York: W.W. Norton and Company.

Wilder, T. (1927). *The bridge of San Luis Rey*. New York: Albert and Charles Boni.

VIII. Jesus Crucified

Jamison, K. (1995). *An unquiet mind.* New York: Random House.

Selzer, R. (1982). *Letters to a young doctor.* New York: Simon and Schuster.

IX. Jesus Talks with a Samaritan Woman

Livingston, G. (2004). *Too soon old, too late smart: Thirty true things you need to know.* New York: Marlow and Company.

McCloskey, P. (2017). "The rift between Jews and Samaritans." Recovered from the Franciscan Media website on 06/14/2017.

X. Progressive Revelation

"A Few Good Men." (1992). United States: Castle Rock Entertainment.

Baha'u'llah. (1990). *Gleanings from the writings of Baha'u'llah.* United States Baha'i Publication Trust,

Potok, C. (1967). *The chosen.* New York: Simon and Schuster.

References

Yalom, I. (2003). *The gift of therapy: An open letter to a new generation of therapists and their patients.* New York: Harper Perennial.

_____. (1980). *Existential therapy.* New York: Basic Books.

XI. Jesus Before Pilate

Bennett, W., Editor. (1993). *The book of virtues.* New York: Simon and Schuster.

Peck, S. (1983). *People of the life: The hope for healing human evil.* New York: Simon and Schuster.

Yalom, I. (1989). *Love's executioner and other tales of psychotherapy.* New York: Basic Books, Inc.

Epilogue: Six Views of the Good Life

Frank, J. (1961). *Persuasion and healing: A Comparative study of psychotherapy.* Baltimore, MD: The Johns Hopkins Press.

James, W. (2017). Recovered from https://www.brainyquote.com/search_results.htmlq=William +James on 06/23/2017.

Martin, M. (1989). *Everyday morality: An introduction to applied ethics*. Belmont, CA: Wadsworth Publishing Company. Recovered from Aristotle (1989). *Ethics*. Translated by J.A.K. Thompson and Hugh Tredennick. New York: Penguin.

Nagel, T. (1970). *The possibility of altruism*. Princeton, NJ: Princeton University Press.

Robinson, D. (2017). *Great ideas of philosophy (2nd edition)*. "Four theories of the good life." Chantilly, VA: The Teaching Company.

Troyat, H. (1967). *Tolstoy* (Translated by N. Amphoux). New York: Doubleday.

References

Other Books by Max Malikow

Being Human: Philosophical Reflections on Psychological Issues

Buried Above Ground: Understanding Suicide and the Suicidal Mind

Death: Reflections on the End of Life and What Comes After

It Happened in Little Valley: A Case Study of Uxoricide

It's Not Too Late! Making the Most of the Rest of Your Life

Living When a Young Friend Commits Suicide (co-authored with Earl A. Grollman)

Mere Existentialism: A Primer

Philosophy 101: A Primer

Philosophy Reader: Essays and Articles for Thought and Discussion (editor)

Profiles in Character: Twenty-Six Stories to Instruct and Inspire Teenagers

Suicidal Thoughts: Essays on Self-Determined Death (editor)

Teachers for Life: Advice and Methods Gathered Along the Way

The Human Predicament: Towards an Understanding of the Human Condition

www.ingramcontent.com/pod-product-compliance
Lightning Source LLC
Chambersburg PA
CBHW071744090426
42738CB00011B/2560